Masterpieces of Art

Neil Morris

MOSES

A life in pictures

BOOK HOUSE

Published in the Great Britain in 2004 by
Book House, an imprint of
The Salariya Book Company Ltd
25 Marlborough Place, Brighton, BN1 1UB

Copyright © 2003 McRae Books Srl

Printed and bound in Italy by Artegrafica, Verona
The series "Art Revelations"
was created and produced by McRae Books Srl
via Borgo Santa Croce, 8 – Florence (Italy)
info@mcraebooks.com
Publishers: Anne McRae and Marco Nardi

Series Editor: Loredana Agosta
Art History consultant: Roberto Carvalho de Magalhães
Text: Neil Morris
Illustrations: Studio Stalio (Alessandro Cantucci, Fabiano Fabbrucci, Andrea Morandi)
Graphic Design: Marco Nardi
Picture Research: Loredana Agosta
Layout: Marco Nardi
Editing: Anne McRae
Repro: Fotolito Toscana, Florence

opposite top:
Moses on Mount Sinai, Ravenna, San Vitale

opposite bottom:
LUCA SIGNORELLI, *Scenes from the Life of Moses*, Vatican, Sistine Chapel

previous page:
REMBRANDT HARMENSZOON VAN RIJN,
Moses Smashing the Tablets of the Law, Berlin, Gemäldegalerie

Table of Contents

Introduction

Since then, no prophet has risen in Israel like Moses, whom the Lord knew face to face... For no-one has ever shown the mighty power or performed the awesome deeds that Moses did in the sight of all Israel. **Deuteronomy 34:10-12**

Moses was a great Hebrew leader and lawgiver. He is one of the most important figures of the Bible, leading the Hebrews, or Israelites, out of slavery to the Promised Land. He also presented them with the Ten Commandments and many other laws. Moses united the Israelite nation on God's instruction, and later Christians saw him as a prophet who foreshadowed Jesus. The world's artists found inspiration in the miraculous events of his life and created great works of art.

THE ISRAELITES IN EGYPT

When the land of Canaan was threatened with famine, Abraham's grandson Jacob took his family south to Egypt. Historians think the emigration may have taken place during the Egyptian New Kingdom (from about 1570 BC), when a succession of powerful pharaohs ruled over a successful empire. Jacob's son Joseph was a great lord in Egypt, but over the next few hundred years the Israelites became an oppressed people. According to the Bible, Moses rescued them from slavery. The Qur'an also tells of Musa (Moses) and his dealings with the pharaoh.

MOSES STRIKING THE ROCK AND THE GATHERING OF MANNA

Agnolo Bronzino
1540–43
Eleonora's Chapel,
Palazzo Vecchio,
Florence (Italy)

The Italian artist Agnolo Bronzino (1503–72), decorated this wall of a private chapel with two scenes showing the Israelites receiving the gifts of food and water during their wandering in the desert. On the left, Moses (1) strikes a rock with his staff from which water flows (2). Rays of light appear as Moses' 'horns' (3). One Israelite (4) puts his lips to the flowing water, while a mother (5) dips in a dish for her crying baby (6). The other fresco shows the Israelites collecting manna. A young man (7) is bent beneath a large jar of manna, while a woman (8) fills a bowl and others allow the food to fall into their garments (9). The two scenes also appear on pages 18–20. Alessandro Allori painted the two Angels with a Chalice and a Globe (10).

EXODUS FROM EGYPT

Moses led the Hebrews out of slavery in Egypt. He took them across the Sinai Desert (a 40-year journey) to Canaan, the 'Promised Land'. During this long journey the Hebrews wandered in the desert and suffered many hardships. However Moses, through God's intervention, helped the people and in some episodes of the Bible, miraculously provided them with food and water.

Above: This reconstruction of a wall painting from a 19th-century BC Egyptian tomb, shows a group of Semitic nomads, probably Israelites from Canaan, with their belongings trading with Egyptians (with red skins).

In this painting by Joos van Wassenhove (active 1460–80), Moses holds the tablets on which God's laws are engraved in Hebrew.

MOSES, THE LAWGIVER

Moses is the dominant character in the first five books of the Bible – *Genesis*, *Exodus*, *Leviticus*, *Numbers*, and *Deuteronomy*. Jewish people call these books the *Torah* (or Law). Christians refer to them as the *Pentateuch* (meaning 'five scrolls'). They were traditionally thought to have been written by Moses, but scholars now believe they were compiled from several later texts. The books of *Exodus* and *Deuteronomy* concentrate on the laws and rules for living which God told Moses to pass on to his people. These laws, including the Ten Commandments, are still followed by Jews, and many are also important for Christians.

THE EXPOSITION OF MOSES
Nicolas Poussin
c 1654
Ashmolean Museum, Oxford (England)

The French painter Nicolas Poussin (1594–1665) painted this scene of Moses being set adrift on the waters. Moses' mother, Jochebed (1), places the papyrus basket containing the infant Moses (2) in the waters of the Nile (3). To the right an allegorical figure (4) representing the Nile or a river god can be seen resting on a sculpture of a sphinx (5), a creature half human and half lion which symbolised power in ancient Egypt. Moses' father, Amram (6), who walks away in grief, is followed by Moses' older brother Aaron (7). Moses' sister, Miriam (8) in the centre of the painting, points to the Egyptian women (9) who have come to bathe in the river. In this episode of Moses' life Miriam played a very important role. She followed the basket drifting in the river making sure that the pharaoh's daughter found it. She also suggested to the pharaoh's daughter that the child be brought to a Hebrew nurse (who was actually Moses' mother) for care.

Saved from the Waters

When she saw that he was a fine child, she hid him for three months. But when she could hide him no longer, she got a papyrus basket for him... Then she placed the child in it and put it among the reeds along the bank of the Nile. His sister stood at a distance to see what would happen to him.
Exodus 2:1-4

Moses was born at a time when the pharaoh had ordered the drowning of all the Hebrews' newborn sons. Moses' mother hid him until he was three months old, then she laid him in a basket and left it among the bulrushes of the River Nile. The baby was found by the pharaoh's daughter. Moses' sister Miriam, who stood watch nearby, suggested that he could be nursed by a Hebrew woman. The princess agreed, and Miriam rushed off to fetch her mother. In this way Moses was reunited with his mother until he was old enough to be taken into the Egyptian court.

THE BIRTH OF MOSES
The Hebrew Jacob, the grandson of Abraham, took his family from Canaan to Egypt when famine struck. Jacob's sons were to form the Twelve Tribes of Israel. Moses was born into the tribe of Levi, Jacob's third son. Towards the end of the 1300s BC, the Pharaoh (probably Seti I or Rameses II) decided there were too many Hebrews in Egypt. He ordered that all Hebrew baby boys be killed, which caused Moses' mother to hide him.

This ancient Egyptian woman is holding a long-stemmed papyrus plant. The bulrushes among which the infant Moses was hidden were probably the stems of this plant which grew abundantly along the banks of the River Nile.

THE PHARAOH'S DAUGHTER
While bathing in the Nile River, the pharaoh's daughter saw the basket floating among the reeds. She sent one of her attendants to fetch it. When she opened it, she found the infant Moses inside. According to the Bible, he was crying and she felt sorry for him. Then, the pharaoh's daughter, with the help of Moses' sister, paid to have him nursed. After the infant had grown older, he was taken back to the pharaoh's daughter who named him Moses, which means 'I drew him out of the water'.

Moses is brought to the pharaoh's court by his daughter and her servants in a painting by the artist Sir Lawrence Alma Tadema (1836-1912).

In the Pharaoh's Court

...Pharaoh's daughter took him and brought him up as her own son. Moses was educated in all the wisdom of the Egyptians and was powerful in speech and action.
Acts 7:21–22.

According to tradition, Moses spent two years with his mother before the pharaoh's daughter took him back to the royal court. Moses was raised and educated with the care of an Egyptian prince. There is no mention in the Bible of this part of Moses' life. Tales about Moses' childhood are found in the Midrash, a collection of Jewish texts which were written to help explain the Bible to readers.

THE TRIAL OF MOSES BY FIRE
Giorgione
c 1502–05
Uffizi Gallery, Florence (Italy)

In this painting by the Venetian artist Giorgione (c 1477–1510), Moses (1) is shown as a very young baby, reaching out for a burning coal from the left-hand dish. The other dish (2) held cherries and/or rubies and other jewels. The Pharaoh (3) watches from his throne, the side of which shows a carved relief (4). The young men holding the trial dishes (5) are dressed in 16th-century clothing, while other courtiers and advisers (6) have an oriental look. One old man (7), perhaps a soothsayer, looks at the pharaoh to gage his reaction. The scene, including the village (8) in the background, is flooded with light which lends the painting an air of enchantment.

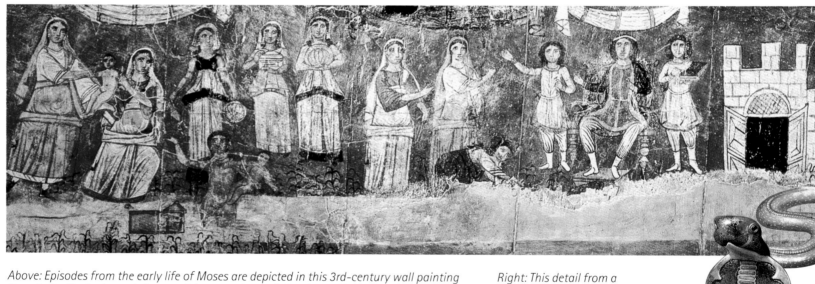

Above: Episodes from the early life of Moses are depicted in this 3rd-century wall painting from Syria. On the lower left, one of the attendants of the pharaoh's daughter takes Moses out of the basket. The pharaoh's daughter then hands the infant to Moses' mother (far left), to be nursed. In the centre, the pharaoh's daughter presents Moses to the pharaoh seated on the right. The young Moses kneels down before the pharaoh.

Right: This detail from a pharaoh's crown shows the cobra goddess of Lower Egypt (the Nile delta region) and the vulture goddess of Upper Egypt.

A THREAT TO EGYPT

According to Hebrew legend, the young Moses trampled playfully on the pharaoh's crown at the Egyptian court. The Egyptian ruler's advisers were concerned since the pharaoh had dreamed that a child would threaten his realm. The child was then given a test to see if he really was a threat to the empire. Two dishes were placed before him, if he chose to grasp the one containing burning coal, he would be seen as innocent. When Moses did just this, he put his burned fingers to his mouth. Legend said that this caused him to stammer in later life. After passing the test, he was accepted at court and held in high regard. Though this episode does not appear in the Bible, it became a popular theme for artists.

In his painting of c 1647, Nicolas Poussin placed the wilful Moses between the Pharaoh and his daughter. He shows the havoc that the simple, playful act has caused among the Egyptian courtiers.

Below: This detail of a mosaic in Venice, Italy, shows Moses being welcomed by Jethro and two of his seven daughters.

Moses in Midian

One day, after Moses had grown up, he went out to where his own people were and watched them at their hard labour. He saw an Egyptian beating a Hebrew... Glancing this way and that and seeing no one, he killed the Egyptian and hid him in the sand. ...When the Pharaoh heard of this, he tried to kill Moses, but Moses fled from Pharaoh and went to live in Midian... Exodus 2:11–15

Moses spent the first 40 years of his life in the Egyptian court. It is believed that during this time he learned somehow that he was Hebrew. This would explain why he killed the Egyptian who was beating a Hebrew slave. Moses then fled to the land of Midian (the north-

SCENES FROM THE LIFE OF MOSES
Sandro Botticelli
1481–82
Vatican, Sistine Chapel

Florentine artist Sandro Botticelli (1445–1510) was summoned to Rome by Pope Sixtus IV in 1481 to decorate the walls of the Sistine Chapel (named after the pope) with scenes depicting the lives of Moses and Christ. In this fresco painting, Botticelli depicts eight distinct scenes from the life of Moses, five of which are shown on the left. The scenes can be read in a circular pattern, starting in the bottom right-hand corner. Moses, dressed in bright yellow, strikes the Egyptian (1), who is helped by a woman (2). Moses then flees to Midian (3) where he drives out the shepherds (4) and draws water for the daughters of Jethro (5) from the well (6) and waters their flock (7). The remaining three scenes (not shown on the large painting) occur later in Moses' life. In the upper left corner, God appears to Moses in the burning bush on Mount Horeb and Moses removes his sandals (see pages 12–13). In the last scene of this painting Moses frees his people from slavery and leads them out of Egypt (see pages 16–17).

Below: This detail from a wall painting by Perugino in the Sistine Chapel, shows Moses' wife Zipporah and two of his sons. Moses named his first-born Gershom, from the Hebrew word for 'stranger'. This was because Moses felt like a foreigner in the land of Midian. The other son was named Eliezer, which means 'my God is helper', since God saved Moses from the pharaoh.

western coastal region of modern Saudi Arabia) to escape from the pharaoh who wanted to have him killed. Moses spent the next 40 years of his life in Midian where he was to marry the daughter of a Midianite priest and become a father.

THE DAUGHTERS OF JETHRO
One day Moses came to rest by a well in Midian where the daughters of Jethro, a Midianite priest, had come to draw water. Some shepherds came along and tried to drive the women away but Moses came to their rescue, drew water for them, and watered their flock. When Jethro's daughters returned home they told their father how an Egyptian man had come to their rescue at the well. Jethro ordered his daughters to invite Moses to their home as a sign of his gratitude. Moses accepted Jethro's invitation and stayed in his home. Jethro then gave Moses his daughter Zipporah in marriage. Zipporah gave birth to two sons. During this time, while Moses lived in Midian, the Israelites suffered great hardship as slaves in Egypt.

God Appears to Moses

… The angel of the Lord appeared to him in flames of fire from within a bush. Moses saw that though the bush was on fire it did not burn up. … God called to him from within the bush, "Moses! Moses!" And Moses said, "Here I am." **Exodus 3:2-4**

One day, when he was looking after his father-in-law Jethro's flocks, Moses saw a bush burning on Mount Horeb. As he approached, Moses heard the voice of God coming from the bush. The voice said that he must go back to Egypt to help his people, the enslaved Israelites. "You will bring them out of their misery," God told Moses, "to a land flowing with milk and honey." This was the land that had earlier been promised to Moses' ancestor, Abraham.

This miniature comes from a 13th-century French illuminated manuscript. Moses is shown in the act of removing his shoes. Moses, known as Musa, is also a major prophet for Muslims. The tradition of removing shoes in a holy place has continued in the practice of Islam.

THE BURNING BUSH

According to the Bible, the voice of God told Moses not to come any closer to the burning bush. Then Moses was told to remove his shoes, since the place where he was standing was holy ground because of the presence of God himself. The miraculous nature of Moses' experience, or vision, on Mount Horeb was that the bush burned but was not consumed. Fire was often used in the Bible to symbolise the presence of God. Though the Book of Exodus has the 'angel of the Lord' appearing within the bush, many medieval artists chose to show a figure of God instead (above).

MOSES BEGINS HIS MISSION

God revealed his name to Moses saying that he was "I Am Who I Am," or Yahweh, the god of his ancestors. God instructed Moses to return to Egypt and free his people. Moses begged God to send someone else saying that he was not an eloquent speaker. God became angry and instructed Moses to appoint his brother Aaron as his spokesman. Moses then gathered his family and began his journey to Egypt. On the way he was reunited with Aaron.

This illustration from a 4th-century Jewish text shows three scenes. Moses meets Aaron and they embrace in the top scenes. Below, Moses, with Aaron's help, explains to the elders of the Israelites how God has given him a mission and proves it by turning Aaron's rod into a snake.

THE BURNING BUSH
(Central panel of a triptych)
Nicolas Froment
1476
Cathedral of St Sauveur,
Aix-en-Provence (France)

The French painter Nicolas Froment (c 1435–86) was commissioned to paint this work by the Duke of Anjou. In it, Moses (1) shields his eyes and at the same time removes his shoes. The winged angel (2), holding a scepter (3), stands to one side. Moses' sheep (4) continue to graze, watched over by an attentive dog (5). The most remarkable image in this picture is that of the Virgin Mary (6) and baby Jesus (7) in the circle of flaming rose-bushes (8). In the Middle Ages the cult of Mary became more important and the unconsumed burning bush became a symbol of her. Both the white rose and the mirror (9) in Christ's hand are also symbols of Mary.

The Ten Plagues of Egypt

Then the Lord said to Moses, "... I will harden Pharaoh's heart, and though I multiply my miraculous signs and wonders in Egypt, he will not listen to you. Then I will lay my hand on Egypt and with mighty acts of judgment I will bring out my divisions, my people the Israelites."
Exodus 7:1-4

Moses was ordered by God to return to Egypt. He and his brother Aaron were to tell the Pharaoh that he must let the Israelites go. When the pharaoh refused to allow this, God sent ten plagues on Egypt. First the Nile's waters turned into blood; then there were swarms of frogs, gnats, and flies; these were followed by cattle pestilence, festering boils, hail, locusts, and darkness. The tenth plague was the most terrible: death to all first-born Egyptian children and animals.

This illustration from a 14th-century Hebrew manuscript from Spain shows the plague of frogs, gnats, flies, and the death of the livestock.

Aaron's rod magically turned into a snake.

The Pharaoh Refuses

Moses and Aaron went to the pharaoh and asked him to let the people go, as God had commanded. When the pharaoh asked to see a miracle, Aaron threw down his rod, or staff, and it turned into a snake. The Egyptian magicians did the same, but Aaron's snake swallowed theirs up. Even after seeing this, the pharaoh was still not convinced. The next day Moses returned and used the same rod to turn the waters of the Nile into blood. This too failed to convince the pharaoh. Then God sent nine more plagues onto Egypt. After the last one, the pharaoh finally agreed to let the Israelites go free.

Below: Although the pharaoh witnessed terrible and miraculous deeds, God hardened his heart.

The Ten Plagues of Egypt

1. The waters of the Nile changed into to blood.
2. Frogs came up from the Nile and covered all of Egypt.
3. All the dust of Egypt turned into gnats which attacked men and animals.
4. Swarms of flies covered and ruined the land of Egypt.
5. A plague killed all of the Egyptians' livestock.
6. The Egyptians suffered from boils, painful swellings on their bodies.
7. Egypt was struck by a terrible hail storm.
8. Locusts covered the land and devoured all of the crops and fruit.
9. Egypt was plunged into darkness for 3 days.
10. All the firstborn Egyptians were killed, including the first-born among the Egyptians' cattle.

God said, "About midnight I will go throughout Egypt. Every firstborn son in Egypt will die, from the first born son of Pharaoh,...to the first born son of the slave girl,...and all the firstborn of the cattle as well" (Exodus 11:5).

The First Passover

Before the tenth plague, God told Moses what the Israelites must do. Each family was to sacrifice a lamb and smear its blood on the lintel and doorposts of their houses. Then they were to roast a lamb or kid and eat it with unleavened bread and bitter herbs. During the meal they were to be ready to leave. When killing the first-born Egyptians, God's destroying angel would pass over and spare the Israelite houses. The blood of the lamb was their salvation. This was the origin of the annual Jewish festival of Passover.

FEAST OF THE PASSOVER
(Altarpiece of the Holy Sacrament)
Dieric Bouts, the Elder
1464-67
Church of St Peter, Louvain (Belgium)

Dieric Bouts (c.1415–75) was the official painter of the city of Louvain (Flemish Leuven), in present-day Belgium. This painting appeared on an altarpiece, and on a smaller scale it repeats the scene of the Last Supper (Christ's final Passover meal with his disciples) on the central panel. The six figures stand around a square table (1), ready to leave at any moment. The paschal (or Passover) lamb (2) became a symbol of the Israelites' salvation and was later associated with Jesus. Wild lettuce (3) and unleavened bread (4) also lie on the table. The central male figure wears the pointed hat (5) that Jews in Christian and Muslim lands wore during the Middle Ages. Like the others, the man on the left has his cloak belted (6), his staff (7) to hand, and is wearing shoes (8). These were God's instructions.

Crossing the Red Sea

Then Moses stretched out his hand over the sea... and all that night the Lord drove the sea back with a strong east wind and turned it into dry land. The waters were divided, and the Israelites went through the sea on dry ground... **Exodus 14:29-30**

After the tenth plague, the pharaoh agreed to let the Israelites leave. This was the start of the great Exodus, or flight from Egypt, led by Moses on God's instructions. He took them through the desert toward waters traditionally identified as the Red Sea. They were followed by an army of Egyptians, since the pharaoh regretted losing all his Hebrew slaves. When Moses stretched his hand over the sea, the waters parted and the Israelites crossed on the dry sea bed. The Egyptian horsemen and charioteers followed, but were all drowned when Moses caused the waters to flow back into place.

The Egyptians urged the people to hurry and leave the country. "For otherwise," they said "we will die!" So the people took their dough before the yeast was added, and carried it on their shoulders... (Exodus 12:33-34).

THE ISRAELITES ON THE BANK OF THE RED SEA
Frans Francken II, 1621
Hamburg Kunsthalle, Hamburg (Germany)

The Flemish artist Frans Francken II (1581-1642), best known for landscape paintings, painted this colourful scene of the Israelites after they had crossed the sea. Here the multitude of Israelites (1) is depicted resting on dry land as the Egyptian horsemen (2) drown in the sea (3). Above the sea there is the pillar of fire (4) which gave the Israelites light through the night. In the centre, an honour guard with a red garment (5) stands over a coffin containing the bones of Joseph (6). God had instructed Moses to take the bones of Joseph because Joseph had made the Israelites promise to take them when God delivered the people from Egypt. The gold and silver objects (7) that were taken from the Egyptians are also shown in this scene.

THE EXODUS

During the night of the tenth plague, the pharaoh ordered Moses and Aaron to take the people and leave Egypt. So the Israelites took their unleavened bread, gathered their clothing, and took the Egyptians' gold and silver objects as Moses had instructed. The Israelites with their flocks and herds began their journey from Egypt. According to the Bible, 'there were about six hundred thousand men on foot, besides women and children'.

THE PHARAOH'S ARMY
When the pharaoh learned that all the Israelites had left Egypt, he changed his mind and led his army after them. Moses and the Israelites were guided through the wilderness by God. By day they followed a pillar of cloud, and at night a pillar of fire gave them light. After the Israelites had crossed the sea on dry ground, Moses stretched out his hand and the waters flowed back into place at dawn. The sea then engulfed the Egyptian soldiers who were racing towards it on their chariots. The Bible says that the entire Egyptian army drowned.

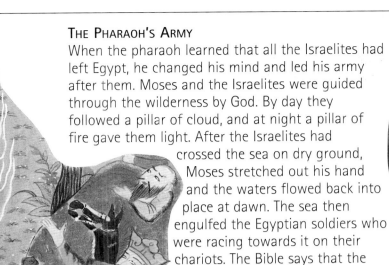

This 15th-century Muslim illustration shows Musa, or Moses, stretching out his hand as he watches the pharaoh's army drown in the sea.

THE SONG OF MIRIAM
After the successful crossing, Moses' sister Miriam led the celebrations. Miriam was a prophetess and was respected by the people. She took up her tambourine, and the Israelite women danced and joined in with Miriam's song: 'Sing to the Lord, for he is highly exalted. The horse and its rider he has hurled into the sea.'

Bronze figure of Miriam and her tambourine from the East Doors of the Baptistery in Florence. The doors were made by Lorenzo Ghiberti (1378-1455). They were so beautiful that Michelangelo called them the Gates of Paradise.

The Gathering of Manna

Then the Lord said to Moses, "I will rain down bread from heaven for you. The people are to go out each day and gather enough for that day." **Exodus 16:4**

Continuing on their journey to Canaan, the Israelites grew tired of the desert and complained to Moses. At one oasis Moses miraculously made bitter water taste sweet, but the people were also hungry. Then God sent a food called manna for them to eat, along with quail for them to catch and roast. The manna fell to the ground like dew, and the idea of this 'bread from heaven' captured the imaginations of many Renaissance artists.

'Six days you are to gather it, but on the seventh day, the Sabbath, there will not be any.' (Exodus 16:26)

WHAT IS IT?

When the Israelites saw the food from heaven, they did not recognise it and asked, "What is it?" They therefore called it manna (from the Hebrew for 'What is it?'), though the word may also have come from a kind of tree resin. The manna was 'white like coriander seed and tasted like wafers made with honey'. God ordered Moses to tell his people that they were to gather as much as they needed and that they were not to look for manna on the seventh day, the Sabbath. Some Israelites disobeyed. Those who gathered too much found maggots in the manna. Those who went out to gather manna on the Sabbath found nothing.

When the Israelites came to a place called Marah, they could not drink the water there because it was bitter. Then Moses threw a piece of wood into the water, as God commanded him, and the water became suitable for drinking.

THE FALL OF MANNA
Tintoretto
1575–77
Scuola Grande di San Rocco, Venice (Italy)

The Venetian artist Jacopo Robusti (1518–94), known as Tintoretto ('little dyer') depicted this scene on the ceiling of the Scuola, an institution which helped to feed the sick. Through a bright opening in the sky, made clearer by the leaves of a tall tree (1) and surrounded by billowing clouds (2), we see the translucent figure of God (3). Beneath this canopy (4), the Israelites and their sheep (5) wake to a vision. One man (6) holds up a round basket to collect the falling manna, while another (7) reaches out, as if trying to touch the source of this bread from heaven.

The Defeat of the Amalekites

The Israelites were soon faced with another great test. They were attacked by the Amalekites, a nomadic people of the Sinai desert. Moses chose Joshua, a descendent of Joseph, to lead the Israelite defence, while he went to a nearby hill to watch the battle. Whenever Moses raised his arms, the Israelites did well, but when he lowered them, they began losing ground. When they saw that Moses was tiring, his brother Aaron and brother-in-law Hur helped him to hold up his arms. By evening the Amalekites were defeated.

This 15th-century miniature shows the two men supporting Moses' arms, as battle rages against the Amalekites. This ensured victory for the Israelites. Moses is shown with his 'horns' (see page 23).

Drawing Water from the Rock

The Lord answered Moses, "Walk on ahead of the people. Take with you some of the elders of Israel and take in your hand the staff with which you struck the Nile, and go. ... Strike the rock, and water will come out of it for the people to drink." Exodus 17:5-6

The long journey through the desert was hard for the Israelites, and it became a great test for Moses. After receiving manna from heaven, the people again complained that they had no water to drink. Moses turned to God and was given a miraculous solution. The provision of water became another popular subject in art. The miracle was seen by many Christians as a symbol of the spiritual refreshment provided by the Church.

Below: A detail from Lippi's painting showing the people and their animals quenching their thirst.

MOSES BRINGS FORTH WATER OUT OF THE ROCK
Filippino Lippi
c 1500
National Gallery, London (England)

The Florentine artist Filippino Lippi (c 1457–1504) received his early training from his father, Fra Filippo Lippi. In this work, he placed Moses (1) at the centre of the picture. He kneels before the rock and touches it with his staff (2). The figure immediately behind him (3) may be Aaron. Two women in flowing garments (4) discuss the miraculous event, while the Israelites (5) and their animals (6) hurry to quench their thirst at the stream (7) gushing from the rock (see

also the detail on the far right). An ox (8) patiently waits its turn. In the background, we see events leading up to this scene: the Israelites being led out of Egypt (9), and their camp at Rephidim (10). Moses later named the place Massah and Meribah (meaning 'testing and quarrelling').

RECEIVING THE TABLETS OF THE LAW
Raphael and collaborators (School of Raphael)
1518–19
Loggia of Pope Leo X, Vatican, Rome (Italy)

The great Italian painter and architect Raphael (1483–1520) was asked by Pope Leo X to decorate the loggia (a covered passage or arcade open on one side) in the Vatican with 52 scenes from the Bible. In this fresco we see Moses (1) on top of Mount Sinai receiving the Tablets of the Law (2). A cloud of smoke (3) surrounds God (4) and a group of angels (5). Four frightened figures (6) keep their distance as they watch. These three figures may represent Aaron and two of his sons, Nadab and Abihu. God said to Moses "Come up to the Lord, you and Aaron, Nadab, and Abihu, and seventy of the elders of Israel. You are to worship at a distance, but Moses alone is to approach the Lord; the others must not come near. And the people may not come up with him" (Exodus 24:1–2). At the foot of the mountain, the Israelites (7) wait for Moses' return beside the tents (8) of their camp.

Moses Receives the Law

Then Moses led the people out of the camp to meet with God, and they stood at the foot of the mountain. Mount Sinai was covered with smoke, because the Lord descended on it in fire. … The whole mountain trembled violently. …The Lord … called Moses to the top of the mountain. **Exodus 19:17-20**

The events on Mount Sinai represent one of the most important episodes in the life of Moses. In its account of these events, the Bible stresses the unique role played by the prophet. He alone was allowed to speak directly to God and receive divine instructions to be passed on to the people. The Ten Commandments were inscribed on two pieces of stone, the 'Tablets of the Law'. In addition, Moses received a further series of laws, known as the Book of the Covenant.

A gold pendant showing the fertility goddess, Astarte. She was worshipped in Canaan and Egypt.

THE TEN COMMANDMENTS

According to the Bible, the Israelites had been travelling in the desert for three months when they set up camp at the foot of Mount Sinai. This was God's holy mountain, sometimes called Horeb, which is traditionally identified as the mountain called Jebel Musa ('Mount of Moses') in Arabic. When Moses climbed the mountain, God told him that he would return in three days' time. On the third day a thick cloud covered Mount Sinai, and there was thunder and lightning. Then there was a loud trumpet blast, and the Israelites shook with fear. When Moses went back up the mountain, God gave him the Ten Commandments to take to his people. He then told Moses of many other laws that the Israelites were to obey. These were rules about the everyday lives of ordinary people. They are still of immense importance to the Jewish people.

A carved stone representation of Baal from Syria. The word 'ba'al' in ancient Hebrew meant 'owner' or 'lord'. Baal controlled the rains, seasons, and world order.

In this sculpture by Pierre Francavilla (1554-1615), Moses is shown with two small horns on his head. The tradition of Moses' horns began when the Hebrew for 'rays of light' was mistranslated as 'horns'.

"YOU SHALL HAVE NO OTHER GODS BEFORE ME"

In the land of Canaan many gods and goddesses were worshipped. The most important god was El, the god of creation. His son Baal, the weather god, who brought the rains, was also widely worshipped along with many other gods and goddesses. Baal's partner was Astarte, a fertility goddess, who was often represented by or with a sacred tree or a cow. The Ten Commandments that God gave to Moses established the laws the Israelites' religion and banned the worship of many gods. Moses is considered the founder of Judaism, the oldest monotheistic religion (a religion with the belief in one god). God said to Moses: "I am the Lord your God, who brought you out of slavery. You shall have no other gods before me." The belief in one God is also central to Christian and Muslim belief.

THE ADORATION OF THE GOLDEN CALF
Nicolas Poussin
c 1634
National Gallery, London (England)

The French painter Nicolas Poussin (1594–1665) was active mainly in Rome. During the 1630s he turned to Old Testament subjects. In this painting, the golden calf (1) looks more like a bull; bulls were also considered sacred in ancient Egypt and Canaan. It stands on a garlanded altar (2) on top of a pedestal.

White-robed Aaron (3) appears to direct the celebrations, as revellers (4) dance around the idol. They form a chain of interlinked movement, as if dancing on a stage. Other bystanders (5) reach out to their new god. In the foreground, a mother (6) looks on entranced. Meanwhile, in the background at the foot of the mountain, a furious Moses (7), accompanied by Joshua (8), raises a tablet high above his head.

Worship of The Golden Calf

So all the people took off their ear-rings and brought them to Aaron. He took what they handed him and made it into an idol cast in the shape of a calf, fashioning it with a tool. Then they said, "These are your gods, O Israel, who brought you up out of Egypt." Exodus 32:3-4

Moses was on Mount Sinai for 40 days receiving the laws from God, and the Israelites grew restless and returned to pagan ways. They asked Aaron to make them a god to lead them further, and he fashioned a golden calf from their jewellery. When people started dancing around the idol, God was angry and told Moses to go back to his people at once. Moses asked God to forgive the Israelites, before turning his own fury on those who had broken the commandment, "You shall not make for yourself an idol."

THE SANCTUARY

Gold told Moses to build a tabernacle, or Tent of Meeting. Inside were to be special items, including an altar, a table, and a seven-branched lampstand. In the inner room, or the Holy of Holies, was to be a chest made of acacia wood, overlaid with pure gold and with two gold cherubs on its lid. This sacred chest, called the Ark of the Covenant (right), was to hold the two Tablets of the Law. The chest and the tabernacle had carrying rods, so that they could be taken from camp to camp as the Israelites continued their journey.

Right: A detail of a 17th-century Italian marble mosaic showing Aaron standing by an altar by the tabernacle. A golden lampstand, or menorah, is placed in front of the curtain which separated the inner room, or Holy of Holies.

MOSES SMASHES THE TABLETS

When Moses saw the people dancing around the golden calf, he was so angry that he threw the stone tablets to the ground. They smashed to pieces. Then he hurled the golden idol into the fire. Finally, he ground it to dust, mixed the gold dust with water and made the Israelites drink it. Later, God told Moses to make two new stone tablets, just like the first ones. When Moses visited him again on Mount Sinai, God wrote the words of the Ten Commandments on the new tablets.

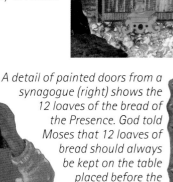

A detail of painted doors from a synagogue (right) shows the 12 loaves of the bread of the Presence. God told Moses that 12 loaves of bread should always be kept on the table placed before the Holy of Holies.

This detail from a painting by the Dutch artist Rembrandt van Rijn (1606-69) shows Moses throwing down the tablets.

THE BRAZEN
SERPENT
*Michelangelo
Buonarroti*
c 1511, Sistine
Chapel, Vatican,
Rome

(Italy)
Michelangelo
(1475-1564)
painted the ceiling
of the Sistine Chapel
in the Vatican between
1508 and 1512. In the
years 1990-1994, the
frescoes on the ceiling
were restored. The layers
of dirt and soot which
covered the frescoes were
removed and brilliant
colours were revealed. On
one of the curving
triangular corner surfaces
on the ceiling the episode
of the Brazen Serpent was
painted. Following God's
instructions, Moses made
a snake out of bronze and
put it on a pole. Moses
again found that his
actions had miraculous
results, all the snake-
bitten Israelites who
looked at the bronze
snake were cured. In this
painting a man (1) holds
up the snake-bitten arm
(2) of a woman towards
the bronze serpent (3). On
the other side venomous
snakes (4) wrap around
the horrified Israelites and
one snake bites a man's
arm (5).

The Brazen Serpent

The Lord said to Moses, "Make a snake and put it up on a pole; anyone who is bitten can look at it and live." ... Then when anyone was bitten by a snake and looked at the bronze snake, that person lived. **Numbers 21:8-9**

The years of wandering in the desert were hard for the Israelites, and for Moses. First his sister Miriam died at Kadesh, and her death was followed by that of Aaron. The people grew more and more restless. They complained about God and Moses, once again saying "Why have you brought us out of Egypt to die in the desert?" God punished them by sending a plague of poisonous snakes. When the people repented and begged Moses to pray to God for them, the prophet was given a miraculous solution.

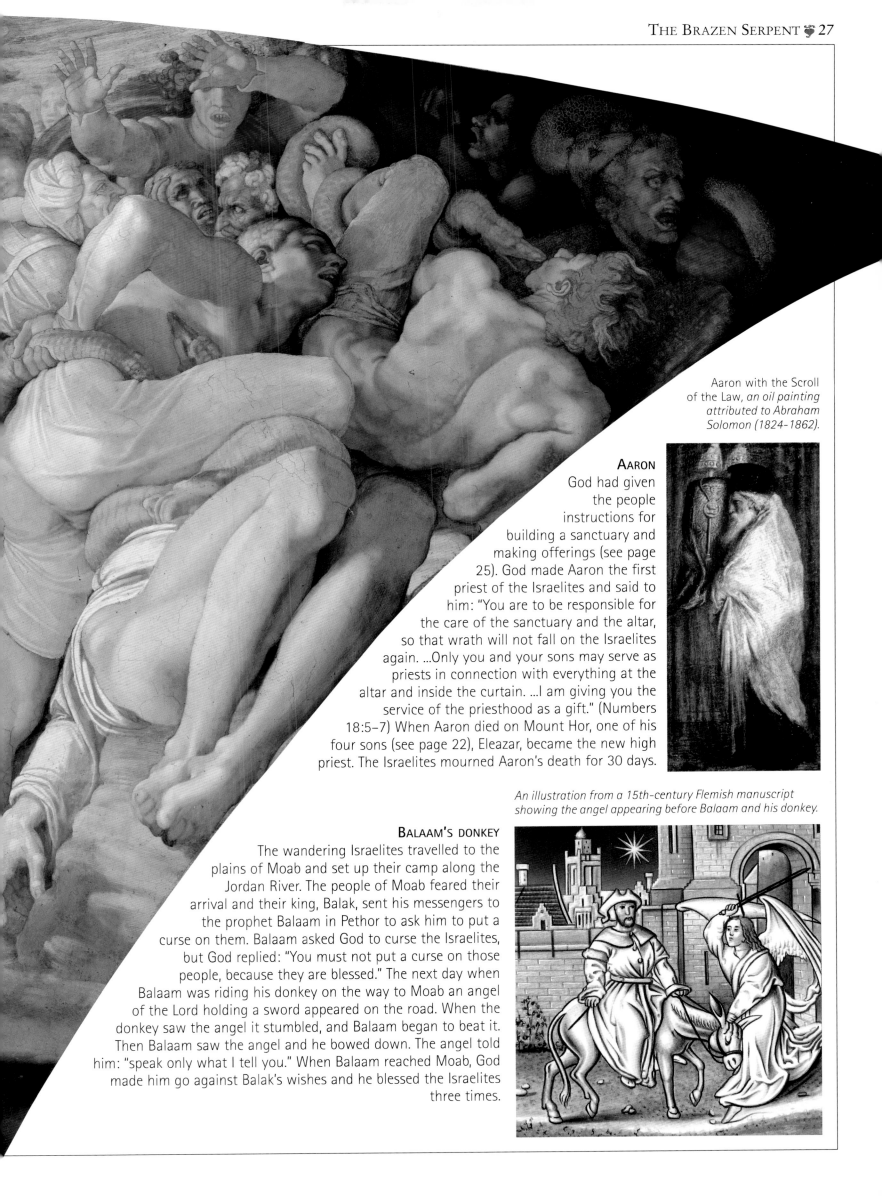

Aaron with the Scroll of the Law, an oil painting attributed to Abraham Solomon (1824-1862).

AARON

God had given the people instructions for building a sanctuary and making offerings (see page 25). God made Aaron the first priest of the Israelites and said to him: "You are to be responsible for the care of the sanctuary and the altar, so that wrath will not fall on the Israelites again. ...Only you and your sons may serve as priests in connection with everything at the altar and inside the curtain. ...I am giving you the service of the priesthood as a gift." (Numbers 18:5-7) When Aaron died on Mount Hor, one of his four sons (see page 22), Eleazar, became the new high priest. The Israelites mourned Aaron's death for 30 days.

An illustration from a 15th-century Flemish manuscript showing the angel appearing before Balaam and his donkey.

BALAAM'S DONKEY

The wandering Israelites travelled to the plains of Moab and set up their camp along the Jordan River. The people of Moab feared their arrival and their king, Balak, sent his messengers to the prophet Balaam in Pethor to ask him to put a curse on them. Balaam asked God to curse the Israelites, but God replied: "You must not put a curse on those people, because they are blessed." The next day when Balaam was riding his donkey on the way to Moab an angel of the Lord holding a sword appeared on the road. When the donkey saw the angel it stumbled, and Balaam began to beat it. Then Balaam saw the angel and he bowed down. The angel told him: "speak only what I tell you." When Balaam reached Moab, God made him go against Balak's wishes and he blessed the Israelites three times.

The Testament, Death and Legacy of Moses

After Moses finished writing in a book the words of this law from beginning to end, he gave this command to the Levites ... "Take this Book of the Law and place it beside the ark of the covenant. ... Assemble before me all the elders of your tribes and all your officials, so that I can speak these words in their hearing and call heaven and earth to testify against them."
Deuteronomy 31:24-28

The Israelites had wandered through the desert for almost 40 years when they approached the River Jordan. Moses, who was now 120 years old, knew that he would not lead them across the river to the Promised Land. After writing down everything that God had told him, Moses called the people together. He said farewell, warning them that there would come a time when they would turn away from their Lord. Then he sang a poetic song in praise of God and blessed the tribes of Israel. After climbing Mount Nebo to look across to the Promised Land, Moses died on the mountain overlooking Canaan.

Left: When the messengers returned from Canaan they brought back a bunch of grapes, figs, and pomegranates.

Below: Honeybees are shown returning to their hives in this illumination. The Promised Land was described as flowing with milk and honey.

THE PROMISED LAND
Moses chose one man from each of the 12 tribes of Israel to explore the land of Canaan, the Promised Land which God had promised them. They were sent to see what the land, the people, and the soil were like. When they came back they said that the land did 'flow with milk and honey' and showed some of the fruit they had picked there. God told Moses: "you will not enter the land I am giving to the people of Israel." Moses climbed Mount Nebo and God showed him the land from a distance. Then Moses died on Mount Nebo.

JOSHUA
Joshua was a mighty warrior who had been chosen by Moses to lead the Israelites against the Amalekites (see page 20). Before dying Moses appointed Joshua his official successor and God chose him to lead the Israelites into the Promised Land. To cross the Jordan River, God told Joshua to send the priests carrying the Ark of the Covenant ahead. As soon as the priests' feet touched the water, the river stopped flowing, and the Israelites walked across on dry ground. Joshua went on to lead the fall of Jericho and conquer Canaan.

This painting by Raphael, from the same series as the painting on pages 22-23, shows the Ark being carried across the Jordan River as a figure representing the river holds back the flow of the waters.

THE TESTAMENT AND DEATH OF MOSES
Luca Signorelli
c 1483
Sistine Chapel, Vatican, Rome (Italy)

The Italian artist Luca Signorelli (c 1441–1523) painted this fresco in the Sistine Chapel. It shows four scenes. In the left foreground, the haloed Moses (1), staff in hand, appoints Joshua (2) his successor. In a separate scene, Moses sits on a throne (3) to read to the people from his book. The central group of figures include women with babies (4) and an enigmatic male nude (5). The prophet is led by an angel (6) as he goes up the mountain to see the Promised Land and view the buildings of Jericho (7) across the river. Moses (8) walks on to a lonely spot, where he dies. There his dead body (9) is found and tended by mourners (10).

The Life of Moses

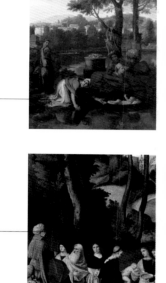

The Pharaoh orders that all male Hebrew babies be killed.

Moses is born in Egypt to Hebrew parents, Amram and Jochebed.

Moses' mother hides him for three months and then places him in a basket in the River Nile.

Moses is found by the Pharaoh's daughter and is given to Jochebed who nurses him for two years.

Moses is brought back to the Pharaoh's daughter and is raised in the Pharaoh's Court.

Moses (at the age of 40) learns that he is Hebrew and kills an Egyptian who was mistreating a Hebrew slave.

Moses flees to Midian and marries Zipporah. Moses' sons are born.

 God appears to Moses in the burning bush.

Moses is reunited with Aaron and returns to Egypt.

Moses and Aaron ask the pharaoh to free the Israelites.

The ten plagues strike Egypt.

Moses (at the age of 80) leads the people out of Egypt and across the Red Sea.

 Moses provides the people with food and water in the desert.

Moses receives the Ten Commandments from God.

Moses returns from the top of the mountain and breaks the tablets and destroys the golden calf.

Moses receives a new set of tablets and they are placed in the tabernacle.

The snake-bitten people are cured by the brazen serpent God instructed Moses to make.

Moses sends the messengers to investigate the Promised Land. Moses appoints Joshua as his successor.

Moses climbs Mount Nebo and sees the Promised Land. Moses dies at the age of 120.

The Lord's Commandments

I am the Lord your God who brought you out of Egypt, out of the land of slavery. You shall have no other Gods before me. You shall not make for yourself an idol...

You shall not misuse the name of the Lord your God... Remember the Sabbath day by keeping it holy. Honour your father and mother...

You shall not murder. You shall not commit adultery. You shall not steal. You shall not give false testimony against your neighbour.

You shall not covet your neighbour's house. You shall not covet your neighbour's wife,... or anything that belongs to your neighbour.

Exodus 20:2-17

Glossary

altar A raised place or structure where religious rites are performed.

Ark of the Covenant The container of the Ten Commandments.

baptistery The part of a church where baptisms take place.

commission A piece of artwork that is requested specifically by a buyer in advance.

Exodus The departure of the Israelites from Egypt, led by Moses.

fresco A technique of painting walls by applying paint to wet plaster.

Hebrew A member of an ancient Semitic people claiming to be descendents of the Old Testament figure, Abraham.

idol An object, often a carved image, that is worshipped as a god.

Israelites A member of the group claiming to be descendants of the Old Testament figure, Jacob.

Judaism The religion of the Jewish people.

Jew A member of the religious community descended from the ancient Israelites.

legacy Objects or instructions handed down by someone when they die, or the state of affairs which they leave behind them.

lintel A horizontal beam over a doorway or window.

locust An insect which travels in swarms and destroy crops.

manna A miraculous food which sustained the Israelites in the wilderness.

Midrash A collection of Jewish texts written to help explain the Bible to readers.

mosaic A design or decoration made up of small tiles of coloured stone or glass.

New Kingdom A period of Egyptian history extending from roughly 1570-1080 BC.

nomadic A tribe of people with no fixed homes, who travel from place to place in search of food and land.

Old Testament The first part of the Christian Bible concerning the origins of the Jewish people.

pagan Someone who believes in a religion with many gods.

papyrus A kind of plant used to make paper in ancient times.

patriarchs The three ancestors of the Hebrew people: Moses, Isaac and Jacob.

pentateuch The first five books of the Old Testament.

pestilence An outbreak of a highly infectious disease.

pharaoh A king of Egypt.

plague A widespread and highly infectious disease.

Presence The Holy Spirit.

Promised Land The land of Canaan, promised by God to Abraham and his people.

Passover A festival to commemorate a story in the Old Testament of when God spared the children of Jewish people and killed those of their Egyptian captors.

prophecy A prediction of what will happen in the future.

prophet Someone who tells a prophecy.

Qur'an The sacred book of Islam.

Renaissance A period at the end of the Middle Ages, when art and literature flourished in Europe.

sanctuary A holy place.

Semitic Another word for Jewish.

synagogue A building for Jewish religious services.

tabernacle A moveable sanctuary in the form of a tent.

Ten Commandments The ten laws passed from God to Moses.

Torah See **pentateuch**

translucent Something that allows light to pass through it.

triptych A set of three pictures or panels, usually connected by hinges, that is often placed on a church altar.

unleavened Made from dough which contains no yeast.

Vatican The administrative centre of the Catholic church in Rome.

Yahweh A Hebrew word for God.

Index

Acknowledgments

The Publishers would like to thank the following photographers and picture libraries for the photos used in this book.
Scala Group, Florence; 1, 4–5, 6–7, 8, 10, 10–11, 12 bottom right, 14, 16, 16–17, 18–19, 19, 20, 20–21, 22–23, 25 bottom right, 27 right, 28, 29. Mondadori x
National Gallery Picture Library, London; 9.
Farabola Foto (The Bridgeman Art Library), Milan; 6, 7, 12–13.
The Metropolitan Museum of Art, Fletcher Fund, 1993 (33.92a) photograph ©1998 The Metropolitan Museum of Art, New York; 3, 26–27.

Artists' Biographies

Sandro Botticelli (born 1445, Florence, died 1510, Florence), whose real name was Alessandro di Mariano Filipepi, was a Renaissance painter best known for his paintings of mythological subjects, such as *The Birth of Venus* and *The Primavera*. He received commissions from the powerful Medici family and major churches. In 1481 he was called to Rome, along with other artists, including Signorelli, to paint the walls of the Sistine Chapel in the Vatican. During the later years of his career, Botticelli turned to small-scale paintings and is believed to have taken many stylistic elements from northern European painters.

Dieric Bouts (born c 1415 Haarlem, died 1475, Louvain) began his career in Haarlem. It is believed that he may have studied with the master Rogier van der Weyden in Brussels early in his career. In 1448 he went to Louvain where he spent the most part of his career, becoming the official painter of the city in 1468. The most famous works of Bouts are from this later period. These include the altarpiece commissioned for the church of St. Peter in Louvain in 1464 and *The Last Judgement* which was left unfinished at his death. Bouts is noted for his way of depicting figures with strong emotion and expressive gestures.

Agnolo Bronzino (born 1503, Monticelli, died 1572, Florence) is known as one of the painters of mannerism (a style which lasted from c 1520 to c 1600). He is also famous for his elegant portraits which set the standards for painters in the following generations. Bronzino took the works of his master, Jacopo da Pontormo, and Michelangelo and Raphael as models for his own style. Bronzino was the court painter to Duke Cosimo I de Medici of Tuscany from 1539 to his death. During this time Bronzino painted religious and allegorical subjects as well as some of his most well-known portraits.

Domenico Fetti (born c 1589, Rome, died c 1623, Venice), received his early training in Rome as a pupil of Ludovico Cardi (1559-1613). He is famous for his religious works set in scenes from everyday life. As a portrait artist he was equally successful, working as the court painter in Mantua, Italy. His style was influenced by that of the Flemish master Peter Paul Rubens who visted Rome between 1600 and 1610. Fetti is often classed as being of the Venetian School due to his presence in Venice for the last two years of his life. Most of his most important works are now in museums in Dresden, St. Petersburg, Paris, Vienna, and Florence

Giorgione (born c 1477 Castelfranco, died 1510, Venice), whose real name was Giorgio Barbarelli, was one of the latter Renaissance painters who helped to develop a new Venetian style. He began his career studying under the master Giovanni Bellini where he developed his use of colour and his way of depicting particular atmospheres. His most popular painting, *The Tempest*, became a model for landscape painters. Giorgione also painted many portraits which impressed many Venetian artists such as Titian, Palma Vecchio, and Lorenzo Lotto.

Filippino Lippi (born c 1457, Prato, died 1504, Florence) was the son of the established painter, Fra Filippo Lippi. After his father's death he entered the workshop of Botticelli and remained there until 1473. Lippi received many commissions from important patrons such as the Medici family of Florence. He was later called to Rome to paint a chapel in the church of Santa Maria Sopra Minerva, which became one of his most praised works. He returned to Florence in the last decade of the 15th century and received other important commissions from the Medici and Strozzi families. His style is thought to have had an important impact on the Tuscan painters of the 16th century.

Michelangelo (born 1475, Caprese, died 1564, Rome), whose full name was Michelangelo di Ludovico Buonarroti Simoni, began his early career as a painter but was also a sculptor, architect, and poet. He is regarded as one of the most influential artists of all time. He spent most of his career in Florence and Rome. During his trip to Rome from 1491 to 1501 he sculpted one of his most famous works, the *Pietà*. After his return to Florence in 1504 he completed the monumental marble sculpture of *David* for the town hall. Soon after he was called back to Rome by Pope Julius who commissioned him the sculpt his tomb and paint the ceiling of the Sistine Chapel. As an architect, he designed many buildings in Florence as well as the dome of St. Peter's Basilica in Rome.

Nicolas Poussin (born 1594, Villers, died 1665, Rome), the French painter, spent the most part of his career in Rome. There he met many influential people and studied classical art (a style which took the art of ancient Greece and Rome as a model). He became one of the greatest painters in Rome at the time. He went to France in 1638 where he served King Louis XIII as court painter for two years. He then returned to Rome and during the later period of his career painted scenes from classical mythology and the Bible. Poussin's style inspired many artists who called themselves Poussinists, they believed that form was more important than colour in painting.

Raffaello Sanzio (born 1483, Urbino, died 1520, Rome) is called Raphael in English. His hometown was one of Italy's centres of culture and learning. At a young age, Raphael became an apprentice to the painter Perugino in Perugia and later went to Florence where he studied the work of Leonardo da Vinci and Michelangelo. In 1508 he was summoned by the pope to Rome, where he would spend the last 12 years of his life. Raphael was commissioned to decorate many rooms of the Vatican Palace and was later appointed the chief architect. He died at the age of 37 and was highly praised by the papal court.

Luca Signorelli (born c 1441, Cortona, died 1523, Cortona) is most famous for his accurate depiction of the human figure. It is believed that he was influenced by the art of Florentine artists during his visit in the 1490s. His masterpiece is found in the cathedral of Orvieto where he painted scenes of *The Last Judgement* and *The End of the World* between 1499 and 1502. These works, which attest to his skill as painter, show muscular figures in various poses and are believed to have inspired Michelangelo.

Tintoretto (born c 1518 Venice, died 1594, Venice), whose real name was Jacopo Robusti, is known as one of the great painters of the late Renaissance and one of the last great Venetian masters. Tintoretto developed his style of by studying the works of Michelangelo. He became a famous painter in Venice and received many commissions from churches, religious groups, Venetian rulers, and the state. Three of his eight children became painters and assisted him in his workshop. Between 1564 and 1587 he painted his masterpiece, a series of biblical scenes on the ceilings and walls of the Scuola di San Rocco in Venice. He became an influential artist noted for his dynamic placement of figures and dramatic use of light.